I0435597

August 26, 2014

MEMORANDUM FOR: The Honorable Alejandro Mayorkas
Deputy Secretary
Department of Homeland Security

Dr. Kathryn Brinsfield
Acting Assistant Secretary and Chief Medical Officer
Office of Health Affairs

FROM: John Roth
Inspector General

SUBJECT: *DHS Has Not Effectively Managed Pandemic Personal Protective Equipment and Antiviral Medical Countermeasures*

Attached for your action is our final report, *DHS Has Not Effectively Managed Pandemic Personal Protective Equipment and Antiviral Medical Countermeasures.* We incorporated the formal comments from the Department in the final report. The report contains 11 recommendations aimed at improving the efficiency and effectiveness of the Department's pandemic preparations. Your office concurred with the intent of all 11 recommendations. We consider Recommendation 9 resolved and closed. Based on information provided in your response to the draft report, we consider the remaining recommendations resolved and open. Once your office has fully implemented the recommendations, please submit a formal closeout letter to us within 30 days so that we may close the recommendations. The memorandum should be accompanied by evidence of completion of agreed-upon corrective actions.

Please email a signed PDF copy of all responses and closeout requests to OIGAuditsFollowup@oig.dhs.gov. Until your response is received and evaluated, the recommendations will be considered open and resolved.

Consistent with our responsibility under the *Inspector General Act*, we will provide copies of our report to appropriate congressional committees with oversight and appropriation responsibility over the Department of Homeland Security. We will post the report on our website for public dissemination.

Please call me with any questions, or your staff may contact Anne L. Richards, Assistant Inspector General for Audits, at (202) 254-4100.

Attachment

Table of Contents

Appendixes

Abbreviations

CBP	U.S. Customs and Border Protection
CDC	Centers for Disease Control and Prevention
COR	contracting officer's representative
DHS	Department of Homeland Security
ECD	Estimated Completion Date
FDA	Food and Drug Administration
FEMA	Federal Emergency Management Agency
FY	fiscal year
HHS	Department of Health and Human Services
IAA	interagency agreement
ICE	U.S. Immigration and Customs Enforcement

OIG-14-129

MCM	medical countermeasures
NCR	National Capital Region
NPPD	National Protection and Programs Directorate
OHA	Office of Health Affairs
OIG	Office of Inspector General
PPE	personal protective equipment
SLEP	Shelf-Life Extension Program
TSA	Transportation Security Administration
USCG	United States Coast Guard
USCIS	U.S. Citizenship and Immigration Services
USSS	United States Secret Service

Executive Summary

The Department of Homeland Security (DHS) supports efforts to develop and execute pandemic contingency plans and preparedness actions as part of the United States Government's pandemic preparedness strategy. A severe influenza pandemic presents a tremendous challenge, which may affect millions of Americans, cause significant illnesses and fatalities, and substantially disrupt our economic and social stability. It is DHS' responsibility to ensure it is adequately prepared to continue critical operations in the event of a pandemic.

In 2006, Congress appropriated $47 million in supplemental funding to DHS for necessary expenses to plan, train, and prepare for a potential pandemic. DHS reported that it spent this funding on personal protective equipment, pandemic research, exercises, and medical countermeasures. The Department and components purchased personal protective equipment and medical countermeasures (specifically, antiviral medical countermeasures) to reduce potential effects of a pandemic and ensure the workforce can continue operations. We conducted an audit of the DHS pandemic preparedness efforts to determine if DHS effectively manages its pandemic preparedness supply of personal protective equipment and antiviral medical countermeasures.

DHS did not adequately conduct a needs assessment prior to purchasing pandemic preparedness supplies and then did not effectively manage its stockpile of pandemic personal protective equipment and antiviral medical countermeasures. Specifically, it did not have clear and documented methodologies to determine the types and quantities of personal protective equipment and antiviral medical countermeasures it purchased for workforce protection. The Department also did not develop and implement stockpile replenishment plans, sufficient inventory controls to monitor stockpiles, adequate contract oversight processes, or ensure compliance with Department guidelines. As a result, the Department has no assurance it has sufficient personal protective equipment and antiviral medical countermeasures for a pandemic response. In addition, we identified concerns related to the oversight of antibiotic medical countermeasures.

We made 11 recommendations that when implemented should improve the efficiency and effectiveness of the Department's pandemic preparations. The Department concurred with the intent of all 11 recommendations.

OIG-14-129

Background

DHS pandemic preparedness strategy includes efforts to develop and execute pandemic contingency plans and preparedness actions. As new threats emerge, DHS must plan and prepare for possible disasters—both natural and manmade. One of these threats is a pandemic resulting from a new influenza virus. A severe influenza pandemic presents a tremendous challenge, which may affect millions of Americans, cause significant illnesses and fatalities, and substantially disrupt our economic and social stability.

According to the Centers for Disease Control and Prevention (CDC), an influenza pandemic can occur when a nonhuman influenza virus is able to transmit efficiently and sustainably from human to human and spread globally.

In the event of any emergency, Federal employees will be expected to continue operations to sustain agency functions. An influenza pandemic is not a singular event, but may come in waves that last weeks or months. It may also pass through communities of all sizes across the Nation and world simultaneously, as demonstrated with the 2009 H1N1 influenza pandemic. The mounting risk of a worldwide influenza pandemic poses numerous potentially devastating consequences for critical infrastructure in the United States.

DHS is responsible for ensuring it is adequately prepared to continue critical operations in the event of a pandemic. The Office of Health Affairs (OHA) serves as DHS' principal authority for all medical and public health issues. OHA provides medical, public health, and scientific expertise in support of DHS' mission to prepare for, respond to, and recover from all threats. OHA leads the Department's workforce health protection and medical oversight activities and provides medical and scientific expertise to support the Department's preparedness and response effort. The Directorate for Management is responsible for implementing the Departmental occupational safety and health program, as well as procurement, property, equipment, and human capital for the Department. Within the Directorate, the Departmental Occupational Safety and Health office integrates safety and health principles into the management of DHS operations, and provides direction and advice to DHS management for occupational safety and health matters.

Both OHA and the Directorate for Management are responsible for organizing pandemic preparations for the Department. These offices provide guidance to DHS components to enable mission readiness and the protection of DHS personnel during a pandemic event. Mission readiness for a pandemic includes having pandemic personal protection equipment (PPE) and antiviral medical countermeasures (MCM) to distribute and dispense during a pandemic. Pandemic PPE is a workplace control measure the DHS workforce may use to prevent infection and reduce the spread of disease. In addition, the distribution and dispensing of antiviral MCM may protect DHS personnel, as well as critical contractors and those within DHS' care and custody who are potentially exposed in a pandemic.

In 2006, Congress appropriated $47 million in supplemental funding to DHS for necessary expenses to train, plan, and prepare for a potential pandemic. DHS reported that it spent this funding on PPE, pandemic research, exercises, and MCM. The Department and components purchased PPE and medication (antiviral MCM) to reduce potential effects of a pandemic and ensure the workforce can continue operations.

Using the appropriated supplemental funding, DHS has maintained PPE and antiviral MCM stockpiles at both the departmental and component levels in preparation for a pandemic response. Specifically, DHS has a PPE stockpile held at a Federal Emergency Management Agency (FEMA) distribution center and multiple component locations. Stockpiles of antiviral MCM are held at a Department of Health and Human Services (HHS) facility and multiple component locations.

We conducted an audit of the DHS pandemic preparedness efforts to determine if DHS effectively manages its pandemic preparedness supply of PPE and antiviral MCM. As part of this audit, we also identified concerns related to oversight of antibiotic MCM, which was outside our audit scope.

Results of Audit

DHS did not adequately conduct a needs assessment prior to purchasing PPE and MCM for pandemic preparedness. DHS did not effectively manage the inventory of pandemic preparedness supplies it purchased. Specifically, it did not have clear and documented methodologies for the types and quantities of PPE and MCM purchased for workforce protection. The Department also did not develop and implement stockpile replenishment plans, sufficient inventory controls to monitor stockpiles, adequate contract oversight processes, or ensure compliance with Department guidelines. As a result, the Department has no assurance that it has sufficient PPE and MCM for DHS employees to continue operations. DHS also has no assurance that the supplies on hand remain effective. As part of our audit work, we also identified concerns related to oversight of antibiotic MCM.

Needs Assessment for Pandemic Preparedness Supplies

DHS did not effectively determine its need for pandemic preparedness supplies prior to purchasing those supplies. Specifically, it did not identify its PPE needs or its needs for antiviral MCM, have clear and documented methodologies for the types and quantities of equipment purchased, have stockpile replenishment plans for either PPE or MCM, or implement sufficient inventory controls to monitor the stockpiles. Much of the PPE DHS purchased is past the manufacturers' date of guaranteed usability and most of the MCM purchased is now nearing the manufacturers' expiration date.[1] As a result, DHS and components may not have sufficient PPE or MCM to provide to the workforce during a pandemic.

Personal Protective Equipment Planning

Prior to purchasing PPE, the Department did not identify the type and quantity needed to continue operations during a pandemic. DHS reported spending $9.5 million on pandemic PPE beginning in 2006 for its headquarters and components, yet did not develop a life cycle management plan.[2] PPE purchases included respirators, surgical masks, gloves, goggles, hand sanitizer, and coverall suits. DHS and components did not have clear and documented methodologies for determining the types and quantities of equipment they needed. By not identifying its needs, the Department cannot be sure its PPE stockpiles are adequate or determine if it has excess supplies on hand. For example:

- The DHS National Capital Region (NCR) pandemic stockpile contains about 350,000 white coverall suits. No justification or related documentation was available to support that this quantity and type of PPE was necessary for pandemic response.

---

[1] Based on the manufacturer's experience, the filter media in the respirators retains its filtration performance in accordance to stated National Institute for Occupational Safety and Health certification for 5 years from the date of manufacture.

[2] A life cycle management plan is a documented process to acquire, maintain, and ultimately dispose of a product or service.

Source: OIG photo
One of 432 pallets of coverall suits at the DHS NCR PPE stockpile.

- The Department has a reported inventory of approximately 16 million surgical masks without demonstrating a need for that quantity of masks.

Source: OIG photo
An aisle of the DHS NCR PPE stockpile containing nitrile gloves, surgical masks, respirators, and coverall suits.

The Department also did not develop alternative use or rotation plans for headquarters and component PPE stockpiles. The Department's entire respirator stockpile has reached, or will soon reach, the manufacturer's date of guaranteed usability. In fact, the Department's own assessment is that the entire PPE stockpile will not be usable after 2015. During site visits, we identified the following:

- The Transportation Security Administration's (TSA) stock of pandemic PPE includes about 200,000 respirators that are beyond the 5-year manufacturer's guaranteed usability. TSA is conducting sampling of its PPE to identify any specific problems with its usability. However, TSA officials said they will maintain existing stock and may use it for "employee comfort."

Source: OIG photo
There were 62,000 surgical masks designated for pandemic use at a TSA warehouse.

- The Department's NCR and component pandemic PPE stockpiles include expired hand sanitizer. Out of 4,982 bottles, 4,184 (84 percent) are expired, some by up to 4 years.

Source: OIG photo
Pallet in DHS NCR stockpile of hand sanitizer that expired in February 2010.

Antiviral Medical Countermeasures Planning

In fiscal year (FY) 2009, OHA purchased approximately 240,000 courses of antiviral MCM on behalf of the Department, without first determining the Department's pandemic needs.[3] After its initial purchases, OHA prepared an acquisition management plan for antiviral MCM, which estimated its requirements. However, OHA did not follow this plan. Instead, OHA acted on a senior-level decision establishing 110 percent coverage of the DHS workforce.[4] The Department has not provided any documentation demonstrating how the current stockpile of approximately 300,000 courses aligns with its pandemic needs.

Since FY 2009, OHA has purchased additional antiviral MCMs without reevaluating the stockpile quantity for reasonableness. OHA conducted periodic data calls to components to identify mission-critical employees. However, OHA did not document how the information was used to ensure its stockpile of antiviral MCM would be sufficient to meet its needs.

---

[3] A course is a series of doses administered to a single individual over a designated period. The DHS antiviral MCM stockpile contains Tamiflu and Relenza.

[4] The DHS workforce includes critical contractors and people under DHS' care and custody. It does not include the United States Coast Guard (USCG) because the USCG maintains its own MCM program and stockpile.

OIG-14-129

Without sufficiently determining its needs, the Department has no assurance it will have an adequate amount of antiviral MCM to maintain critical operations during a pandemic. Also, it cannot ensure previous and future purchases of antiviral MCM are an efficient use of resources. DHS acquired most of its stockpile of antiviral MCM in FY 2009, but did not implement an acquisition management plan that included a strategy for replenishment. Having an acquisition management plan would ensure its stockpile continued to meet its needs. As a result, about 81 percent of its stockpile will expire by the end of 2015 (shown in table 1). DHS recently spent about $760,000 on an additional purchase of 37,000 antiviral MCM courses, yet had still not demonstrated how that purchase met its needs.

OHA is applying for a shelf-life extension with the Food and Drug Administration (FDA) to extend the expiration dates on the antiviral MCM expiring in 2015, specifically Tamiflu, in the DHS stockpile. We applaud their effort and encourage this process, as it reduces the resources needed to replace expiring drugs and would extend their Tamiflu stockpile expiration until 2018. However, OHA has not yet been granted an extension. Even with the extension, this may not fulfill the DHS requirements if a pandemic event occurs.

Table 1. Courses of DHS Antiviral Medical Countermeasures Expiring in 2015

Antiviral MCM	Current Antiviral MCM Stockpile	Antiviral MCM Expiring in 2015	Percent of Antiviral MCM Expiring in 2015
Tamiflu	192,272	192,272	100%
Relenza	103,734	47,472	46%
Totals	**296,006**	**239,744**	**81%**

Source: OIG analysis

Management of Pandemic Preparedness Supplies

DHS did not effectively manage and oversee its inventory of pandemic preparedness supplies, including PPE and antiviral MCM. Specifically, DHS did not keep accurate records of what it purchased and received and did not implement sufficient controls to monitor its stockpiles. As a result, DHS may not be able to provide sufficient pandemic preparedness supplies to its employees to continue operations during a pandemic.

Personal Protective Equipment Oversight

DHS did not have proper oversight of its pandemic PPE supplies. It did not keep records of what it purchased and received, and it has not accurately accounted for how much PPE it currently has in stock. There is departmental guidance on inventory management; however, the Department and components did not establish and maintain accurate inventories in accordance with that guidance. This condition may have existed because the Department and components did not use an inventory system to track and monitor PPE or perform periodic inventories of their PPE stockpiles. For example, the Department lost a secondary PPE stockpile, once located in Washington, DC, containing 25,000 surgical masks and hand sanitizer. A Federal Government office building in Washington, DC received this stockpile in 2009, but officials were unable to locate the stockpile for this audit and reported it as lost. Additionally, at a site visit to the DHS NCR stockpile at a FEMA distribution center, we found inventory discrepancies as seen in table 2.

Table 2. Analysis of DHS National Capital Region Stockpile

Personal Protective Equipment Item	FEMA Distribution Center Inventory Aug. 2013	OIG Verified Count Aug. 2013	Discrepancy
Model 9210 Respirators	Not on Inventory	4,800	4,800
Model 1860 Respirators	919,080	928,320	9,240
Coverall Suits	367,800	356,400	-11,400
Hand Sanitizer (8 oz.)	Not on Inventory	784	784
Protective Goggles	23,214	20,312	-2,902

Source: OIG analysis

We also identified inaccurate inventories at component offices. United States Immigration and Customs Enforcement (ICE), National Protection and Programs Directorate (NPPD), and TSA did not establish an inventory of the initial stock they received from the Department. Subsequent attempts to inventory their pandemic PPE were not accurate. ICE and TSA officials reported unknown quantities of PPE may have been disposed of, but we could not verify this report since the components had not performed an earlier inventory. In fact, at some ICE and United States Secret Service (USSS) locations, PPE was distributed to employees without any tracking or record keeping.

Management of the Department's pandemic PPE has not been effective because responsibility at the departmental level has not been clearly designated. The Directorate for Management and OHA have different interpretations regarding the roles and responsibilities for administration and oversight of DHS' NCR stockpile. Both offices acknowledged that there is no clear delineation of responsibilities necessary to guarantee successful coordination of the management and oversight of pandemic PPE. They have agreed to clarify their roles. Without delineated roles, proper management, accountability, and oversight of the Department's pandemic PPE cannot occur.

Antiviral Medical Countermeasures Inventory Management

DHS decided to pre-position some of its stockpile to component offices in response to the H1N1 influenza pandemic in 2009. OHA pre-positioned approximately 32,000 courses of antiviral MCMs to U.S. Customs and Border Protection (CBP), ICE, USSS, and FEMA locations. OHA did not maintain complete or accurate records of the quantity and shipped location of MCM distributed from the stockpile, and components did not document receipt of MCM.

In 2010, OHA requested component inventories, but did not validate the reported information. OHA cannot account for nearly 6,200 courses of antiviral MCM pre-positioned with the components (see table 3). During our review, we were able to locate more than 4,000 courses of antiviral MCM; however, more than 2,000 courses remain missing.

Table 3. Analysis of OHA and Component Antiviral Medical Countermeasures Inventories

Component	Courses Shipped by HHS	Courses Reported to OHA by Components	Net Adjustments from OIG Validation	Courses Missing
CBP	24,192	20,275	2,040	1,877
FEMA	144	144	0	0
ICE	6,240	5,496	696	48
USSS	1,536	0	1,406	130
Grand Total	**32,112**	**25,915**	**4,142**	**2,055**
Total Unknown to OHA			**6,197**	

Source: OIG analysis

Based on our analysis of antiviral MCM sent to components, OHA and components did not have complete or accurate inventories of pre-positioned antiviral MCM. Specifically, we identified the following:

- OHA sent more than 1,500 courses of antiviral MCM to the USSS headquarters. OHA did not have records of any MCM at USSS because it did not maintain shipment documentation.
- OHA sent 590 courses of antiviral MCM to eight CBP field offices, of which CBP headquarters was unaware because it did not monitor antiviral MCM until 2012.
- At two CBP locations, we found inventory discrepancies including one location that reported 90 courses, but actually had 1,344; and another location reported 330, but actually had 528.
- At three ICE field office locations, 720 courses of antiviral MCM were incorrectly reported to ICE headquarters as destroyed; yet, we identified they were still in possession of these MCM courses.

Interagency Agreement Oversight

OHA had interagency agreements (IAA) with HHS for the storage and logistics of the majority of its antiviral MCM. However, OHA did not ensure proper contract administration and oversight. Specifically, there was no documentation that the contract performance was routinely monitored. Only one inspection was documented during the entire contract period. The most recent contracting officer's representative (COR) was unaware of his appointment and did not fulfill his duties for more than 7 months. This occurred because the program office responsible for designating the COR did not notify the COR of his appointment and responsibilities.

COR oversight is essential to ensuring that goods are received and services are performed in accordance with the statement of work. However, OHA has paid HHS without ensuring it received goods and services. We notified OHA of this problem, and OHA has since designated a COR and issued an appointment letter outlining COR duties and responsibilities.

Antiviral Medical Countermeasures Guidance and Monitoring

OHA issued guidance that pre-positioned antiviral MCM was to be securely stored in remote locations with limited or no immediate access to medical care, properly dispensed, and kept in a temperature-controlled environment. However, CBP, ICE, and USSS did not follow OHA's guidance on pre-positioning antiviral MCM in remote locations, and OHA did not enforce this requirement. Instead, OHA allowed components to store antiviral MCM in major metropolitan areas like Boston, MA; Chicago, IL; Denver, CO; Miami, FL; and Washington, DC. For example, ICE requested that OHA send an equal amount of antiviral MCM to locations nationwide, regardless of the size of the office or of its remote location.

Neither OHA nor components provided documented guidance regarding how to properly secure the antiviral MCM. This contributed to the ineffective management of the antiviral MCM and diminished the Department's ability to continue critical operations during a pandemic. For example, ICE was missing 48 courses of antiviral MCM at two of its locations. ICE headquarters cannot account for what happened to the missing courses of antiviral MCM. We visited one of these offices and found that the medication was in an unsecured office storage room.

In addition to missing antiviral MCM, USSS may have improperly dispensed 130 courses of antiviral MCM to its employees to treat influenza in 2009. USSS could not provide any documentation, as required, to show they were dispensed. OHA officials said components were not authorized to dispense the antiviral MCM. OHA did not maintain records of MCM at USSS, and it may not have provided guidance on proper dispensing protocols to USSS.

OHA also had no assurance that components stored antiviral MCM at the proper temperature and did not monitor components to ensure MCMs were stored in continuously temperature-controlled environments. OHA's 2009 guidance for antiviral MCMs outlined the requirements for storage temperature, but it did not have monitoring requirements for components to ensure the antiviral MCM were stored properly.

Additionally, component headquarters did not issue guidance for their field offices or ensure proper controls were in place to account for the antiviral MCM after it was pre-positioned. Specifically, components did not ensure antiviral MCM were consistently stored at the correct temperatures. For example, at multiple sites we visited, officials said the buildings where antiviral MCM were being stored were not temperature controlled during evenings and weekends. OHA spent approximately $600,000 on the antiviral MCM sent to component field offices. OHA does not have assurance that the pre-positioned antiviral MCM have been properly stored. Therefore, it is in the process of recalling approximately 32,000 courses of antiviral MCM for possible destruction due to concerns about safety and efficacy.

Additional Observation

Although antibiotic MCM was outside the scope of our audit, we have similar concerns regarding the effectiveness of CBP's monitoring of its antibiotic MCM.

During four of our CBP site visits, we observed antibiotic MCM stored alongside antiviral MCM. CBP MCM monitoring relies on the self-reported inventories, which do not contain storage conditions at field offices. This monitoring is insufficient to ensure pre-positioned antibiotic MCM are being stored according to requirements. As a result, the usability of its stockpile of more than 88,000 courses of antibiotic MCM, valued at $5 million, may be questionable.

OHA has agreements in place with most components giving them the responsibility to properly store antibiotics and outlining requirements to maintain the antibiotics. During our audit, we observed inadequate monitoring of storage conditions only at CBP. However, we urge OHA to ensure there is proper management and oversight of the Department's pre-positioned antibiotic MCM and that components comply with all storage requirements.

Recommendations

We recommend that the Deputy Secretary:

Recommendation #1:

Identify and designate an office responsible for the management and accountability of pandemic PPE.

We recommend the office designated for the management and accountability of pandemic PPE:

Recommendation #2:

Develop a strategy for management, storage, and distribution of pandemic PPE.

Recommendation #3:

Implement an inventory system for the current inventory and future inventories of pandemic PPE.

Recommendation #4:

Work with components to establish a methodology for determining sufficient types and quantities of pandemic PPE to align with the department-wide pandemic plan.

Recommendation #5:

Have components implement inventory control procedures for pre-positioned pandemic PPE to monitor stockpiles, track shipments, and ensure compliance with departmental guidance.

We recommend the DHS MCM Working Group and OHA:

Recommendation #6:

Determine requirements of antiviral MCM for the Department to maintain critical operations during a pandemic.

We recommend OHA:

Recommendation #7:

Create an antiviral MCM Acquisition Management Plan to include:
   a) a methodology for determining the ideal quantity of antiviral MCM OHA will stockpile and how frequently it will be reevaluated;
   b) a replenishment plan; and
   c) inventory tracking, reporting, and reconciliation procedures for existing stockpile and new antiviral purchases.

Recommendation #8:

Revise procedures to ensure proper contract oversight by government employees for management of its MCM support service contracts and ensure the contracting officer's representatives follow procedures.

Recommendation #9:

Finalize and issue antiviral MCM guidance on the storage conditions, security, and distribution for antiviral MCM for all components.

Recommendation #10:

Finalize the antiviral MCM recall it has initiated on the CBP, ICE, FEMA, and USSS inventories.

Recommendation #11:

Collaborate with CBP to determine the safety and effectiveness of the antibiotic MCM that have been stored alongside their antivirals.

Management Comments and OIG Analysis

In its response to our draft report, the Department concurred with the intent of all 11 recommendations. It identified issues it believed were not appropriately characterized, which are addressed below. The Department expressed concern that we overemphasized the role of PPE and MCM, which they view as the last in a hierarchy of controls. During the audit, we did review the hierarchy of controls including engineering controls, administrative controls, PPE, and MCM. The audit focuses on PPE and MCM due to the extensive governmental resources dedicated to purchasing materials and drugs in both areas. In addition, according to the DHS Chief Medical Officer, "the MCM Program plays a vital role in protecting our workforce and ensures that the Department's operational and headquarters components have the capability and the resources to continue to fulfill our mission during a major incident." We were unable to include information on engineering controls because the Department could not provide documentation to demonstrate this control was used. According to DHS officials, no funding has been allocated for engineering controls, such as physical barriers. We also considered the potential impact of administrative controls, specifically telework. At the time of our audit, less than 5 percent of DHS employees actually teleworked and approximately 30 percent of DHS employees were in positions that are capable of telework. Many of DHS employees conduct operations, such as passenger screening, that are not suitable for telework. Therefore, while there are alternative controls, we chose to focus on where DHS has invested its resources and on the controls within the hierarchy that would be critical in allowing DHS operations to continue during a pandemic.

In auditing PPE and MCM, the OIG relied on HHS, FDA, CDC, manufacturer information, and DHS's medical, safety and health professionals as outlined in the report. The Department headquarters' entire respirator stockpile has reached, or will soon reach, the manufacturer's date of guaranteed usability. According to a Departmental safety and health official, "although periodic sampling by DHS professional occupational safety and health personnel could establish whether it remained usable, Management has determined the best alternative is to standardize the pandemic PPE supply chain and discontinue headquarters' reliance on current stockpiles and dispose of them by the end of 2015." At the time of the audit, DHS provided no documentation on plans to replace their current PPE stockpile by 2015 and the funding to accomplish such a task. The audit found that DHS and components do not know where PPE is located, how much it has, and the usability of the stockpiles that exist. Although DHS has identified PPE and MCM as the least effective controls, it has invested millions in purchasing these resources without determining the quantities needed for a pandemic response. According to DHS, it is not required under the Occupational Safety and Health Administration to provide PPE supplies to its personnel; however, it has elected to do so in its own planning requirements. DHS should ensure it has sufficient supplies to fulfill its requirements and that the supplies are in working condition.

In addressing MCM, OHA has taken steps with the FDA to use the Shelf-Life Extension Program (SLEP), which can save valuable resources by extending expiration dates on drugs still found to be effective. We applaud their effort and encourage this process, as it reduces the resources needed to replace expiring drugs. However, OHA needs to ensure that it properly identifies the drugs that receive such an extension. OHA improperly identified in its response that it had been granted an FDA extension for its antiviral MCM. The FDA has not approved the specific drugs OHA has in its strategic stockpile that are due to expire next year. During meetings with the Department, they confirmed they did not have an FDA extension for their stockpile.

The plans in place when the audit was initiated were the 2009 H1N1 plans for both the Department and the components. The Department was in the process of updating its pandemic plans, so we were unable to review those as part of this initial audit. The Department's pandemic planning efforts will be addressed in an upcoming audit.

Recommendation #1: Concur. The Office of the Under Secretary for Management designated the DHS Office of the Chief Readiness Support Officer as being responsible for the management and accountability of pandemic PPE effective January 2014. We request that OIG consider this recommendation resolved and closed.

OIG Analysis: The Department's response to this recommendation addresses the intent of the recommendation. This recommendation is resolved and will remain open until the Department provides evidence that the Chief Readiness Support Officer has been designated as being responsible for the management and accountability of pandemic PPE effective January 2014. The Department should also provide a copy of the new policy memo, once implemented.

Recommendation #2: Concur. The DHS Chief Readiness Support Officer issued a Pandemic Logistics Support Plan Charter on May 30, 2014. This charter establishes the framework for the development of a Department pandemic logistics support plan for pandemic PPE. A Pandemic Logistics Integration Team (iTeam) has also been established with representation from DHS Components and pandemic PPE requirements have been drafted. Estimated Completion Date (ECD): September 30, 2014.

OIG Analysis: The Department's response to this recommendation addresses the intent of the recommendation. This recommendation is resolved and will remain open until the Department provides a copy of the strategy for management, storage, and distribution of pandemic PPE developed by the Pandemic Logistics Integration Team. We will close this recommendation upon determining that the evidence provided meets the intent of this recommendation.

Recommendation #3: Concur. Members of the Pandemic Logistics iTeam are reviewing the application of the Department's existing personal property inventory management systems for establishing management and inventory controls for pandemic PPE. The current pandemic PPE inventories are being distributed within DHS where operational requirements can be augmented; remaining items will be surplused in accordance with Federal and Department requirements and standards. ECD: September 30, 2014.

OIG Analysis: The Department's response to this recommendation addresses the intent of the recommendation. This recommendation is resolved and will remain open until the Department provides a copy of the implementation plan including the inventory system for the current inventory and future inventories of pandemic PPE developed by the Pandemic Logistics Integration Team. We will close this recommendation upon determining that the evidence provided meets the intent of this recommendation.

Recommendation #4: Concur. Work is underway. A workgroup has been established under the Pandemic Logistics iTeam to develop PPE requirements using an employee risk based approach supporting work place controls. ECD: September 30, 2014.

OIG Analysis: The Department's response to this recommendation addresses the intent of the recommendation. This recommendation is resolved and will remain open until the Department provides a copy of the workgroup's plan establishing a methodology for determining sufficient types and quantities of pandemic PPE to align with the department-wide pandemic plan. We will close this recommendation upon determining that the evidence provided meets the intent of this recommendation.

Recommendation #5: Concur. This is in the planning stage. A policy and standards workgroup is being established under the Pandemic Logistics iTeam to establish PPE control procedures and standards. ECD: September 30, 2014.

OIG Analysis: The Department's response to this recommendation addresses the intent of the recommendation. This recommendation is resolved and will remain open until the Department provides a copy of the workgroup's plan implementing inventory control procedures for pre-positioned pandemic PPE to monitor stockpiles, track shipments, and ensure compliance with departmental guidance. We will close this recommendation upon determining that the evidence provided meets the intent of this recommendation.

Recommendation #6: Concur. Concur. OHA continues to solicit, receive, and address DHS component MCM needs and requirements as a standing agenda item during the monthly MCM Working Group meeting, and as a key element of the MCM Quarterly Reports, OHA prepares and distributes as part of the MCM program. Additionally, DHS is working with CDC on an interagency process to define antiviral stockpiling needs on behalf of the entire Federal Government. We request that OIG consider this recommendation resolved and closed.

OIG Analysis: The Department's response to this recommendation addresses the intent of the recommendation. This recommendation is resolved and will remain open until the Department provides a copy of the workgroup's plan outlining the determination of requirements of antiviral MCM for the Department to maintain critical operations during a pandemic. We will close this recommendation upon determining that the evidence provided meets the intent of this recommendation.

Recommendation #7: Concur. An MCM Integrated Logistics Support Program has been drafted and is currently in DHS clearance. Completion of the MCM Integrated Logistics Support Program will address all three elements of this recommendation. ECD: September 30, 2014.

OIG Analysis: The Department's response to this recommendation addresses the intent of the recommendation. This recommendation is resolved and will remain open until the Department provides a copy of the Integrated Logistics Support Program addressing all three elements of this recommendation. We will close this recommendation upon determining that the evidence provided meets the intent of this recommendation.

Recommendation #8: Concur in principle. Existing procedures as described in the Homeland Security Acquisition Regulation, Homeland Security Acquisition

Manual, the DHS Office of Procurement Operations contracting officer's representative guidebook and component-specific procedures addressing contracting officer's representative duties and responsibilities are adequate for ensuring proper contract oversight, but these procedures were not followed consistently in the administration of MCM support service contracts. Since OIG identified findings concerning inadequate oversight, OHA has taken steps to ensure that highly qualified contracting officer's representatives are assigned to all MCM support service contracts. These employees provide direct and comprehensive oversight of each aspect of the MCM project including detailed governance over all related contract support. We request that OIG consider this recommendation resolved and closed.

OIG Analysis: The Department's response to this recommendation addresses the intent of the recommendation. This recommendation is resolved and will remain open until the Department provides a copy of the revised procedures to ensure proper contract oversight by government employees for management of its MCM support service contracts and ensure the contracting officer's representatives follow procedures. We will close this recommendation upon determining that the evidence provided meets the intent of this recommendation.

Recommendation #9: Concur. Storage and security guidance MCM standard operating procedures initially released in 2010 have been updated and expanded, and provided to component MCM planners. They have also been posted to the DHS Connect Intranet MCM page. We request that OIG consider this recommendation resolved and closed.

OIG Analysis: The Department's response to this recommendation addresses the intent of the recommendation. The Department provided supporting documentation on storage and security guidance MCM standard operating procedures that have been updated and expanded, and provided to component MCM planners. This documentation was sufficient to close this recommendation. This recommendation is resolved and closed.

Recommendation #10: Concur. The recall is complete. OHA recently received a confirmation letter, dated July 7, 2014, from the HHS storage facility advising that all antiviral lots had been returned. We request that OIG consider this recommendation resolved and closed.

OIG Analysis: The Department's response to this recommendation addresses the intent of the recommendation. This recommendation is resolved and will remain open until the Department provides a copy that all antiviral MCM shipped to the field locations has been returned. There are still 1,071 courses of antiviral MCM sent from the field that have not been returned to the HHS facility. There were five locations that did not return any of the antiviral MCM they were shipped, and there were eight locations that did not return the full amount of the MCM that was originally shipped. This recommendation cannot be closed until OHA locates the remaining courses or documents that those courses have been lost and provides documentation in either case. We will close this recommendation upon determining that the evidence provided meets the intent of this recommendation.

Recommendation #11: Concur. OHA continues to collaborate with all DHS Components to include U.S. Customs and Border Protection, through the MCM Working Group, to validate the safety and effectiveness of MCM. DHS employs the approved SLEP in close coordination with the FDA and the U.S. Department of Defense. To date, ten lots of antibiotic MCM have been submitted to SLEP for testing and of those for which testing has been completed all have been found to remain efficacious resulting in a cost avoidance of $5.1 million to the Department.

In addition to extending the shelf life, the SLEP testing verifies the safety/efficacy of MCM that may have been stored improperly (outside of the manufacturer's temperature range). In one instance, 5,450 bottles of antibiotics were exposed to a temperature spike over 100 degrees Fahrenheit for an unknown duration. The lot was submitted to SLEP to test for continued efficacy. It was found to be still safe and effective for use, and it was returned to the DHS stockpile.

Additionally, on July 7, 2014, OHA provided procedural guidance to DHS Components regarding MCM on measures to ensure the safety and effectiveness of medications, including antibiotics, in the MCM Program. We request that OIG consider this recommendation resolved and closed.

OIG Analysis: The Department's response to this recommendation addresses the intent of the recommendation. This recommendation is resolved and will remain open until the Department provides documentation on how it is validating the safety and effectiveness of the MCM. We will close this recommendation upon determining that the evidence provided meets the intent of this recommendation.

Appendix A
Objectives, Scope, and Methodology

The DHS OIG was established by the *Homeland Security Act of 2002* (Public Law 107-296) by amendment to the *Inspector General Act of 1978*. This is one of a series of audit, inspection, and special reports prepared as part of our oversight responsibilities to promote economy, efficiency, and effectiveness within the Department.

We conducted an audit of the DHS pandemic preparedness efforts to determine if DHS effectively manages its pandemic preparedness supply of PPE and antiviral MCM. To achieve our audit objective, we identified and reviewed applicable Federal laws, regulations, and DHS policies and procedures regarding pandemic preparedness. The audit covered DHS pandemic efforts from FY 2006 through April 2014.

We interviewed DHS officials within the Directorate for Management, the Office of Operations Coordination and Planning, OHA, and some components responsible for pandemic preparedness planning, administration, oversight, and management. Specifically, we met with component officials from CBP, FEMA, ICE, TSA, USCG, NPPD, U.S. Citizenship and Immigration Services (USCIS), and USSS. We also interviewed personnel at HHS.

We met with Department officials to determine which offices were responsible for pandemic preparedness planning, management, and oversight to ensure workforce protection. We interviewed DHS officials within the Directorate for Management, the Office of Operations Coordination and Planning, and OHA responsible for pandemic preparedness planning, administration, oversight, and management. We also met with HHS personnel who conduct the storage and logistics of the DHS antiviral MCM stockpile as part of the IAA. Finally, we interviewed DHS employees from component headquarters and field offices of CBP, FEMA, ICE, TSA, the USCG, NPPD, USCIS, and USSS.

To determine if DHS effectively manages its pandemic PPE, we reviewed what plans and guidance DHS had for the types and quantities of PPE, for the alternative use or rotation of the equipment, and for distribution of PPE to components. We assessed the accuracy of DHS inventories by conducting a judgmental sample of site visits and a physical verification of onsite equipment. Specifically, we visited pandemic PPE stockpiles for the NCR at a FEMA distribution center and at ICE, USSS, TSA, and NPPD locations and documented storage conditions and discrepancies between inventories and quantities onsite. We assessed DHS oversight of its pandemic PPE stockpile by determining how DHS tracked and monitored PPE, conducted periodic inventories of their PPE stockpiles, and delineated the roles and responsibilities between DHS offices. See table 4 for the offices we visited that possessed PPE.

Table 4. Personal Protective Equipment Site Visits

Component	Number of Locations
FEMA	4
ICE	5
NPPD	2
TSA	5
USSS	3

Source: OIG

To determine if DHS effectively manages its pandemic preparedness supply of antiviral MCM, we determined whether OHA created plans for its acquisition and inventory management. We evaluated the guidance OHA issued on appropriate storage and distribution of antiviral MCM. We assessed OHA oversight of its antiviral MCM stockpile by determining how OHA tracked and monitored antiviral MCM, conducted inventories of the antiviral MCM stockpiles, and ensured performance of COR responsibilities. We assessed the accuracy of OHA and component antiviral MCM inventories by comparing their inventories with the shipping data from HHS. In addition, we reviewed the accuracy of component headquarters' inventories of antiviral MCM stockpiled at their offices by conducting a judgmental sample of site visits and a physical verification of the medication on site. Specifically, we visited antiviral MCM stockpiles at an HHS storage facility and at ICE, CBP, NPPD, and USSS locations, and documented storage conditions and discrepancies between inventories and quantities on site. See table 5 for the offices and locations we visited.

Table 5: Medical Countermeasures Site Visits

Component	Number of Locations
CBP	14
FEMA	1
ICE	12
NPPD	1
TSA	1
USCG	1
USCIS	1
USSS	2

Source: OIG

We relied on components and DHS headquarters to provide us counts of their pandemic PPE and antiviral MCM stockpiles, which were not complete and accurate. We performed physical verification by sampling inventories at the headquarters level, as well as at component headquarters and field office locations selected. We also compared original order and shipment information for antiviral MCM with OHA and component inventories and were able to identify quantities that were in undocumented locations or missing. The evidence from testing the inventories through our physical verification during site visits and analysis of data was sufficient and adequate for the purposes of meeting our audit objective and supporting our audit findings.

We conducted this performance audit between July 2013 and April 2014 pursuant to the *Inspector General Act of 1978*, as amended, and according to generally accepted government auditing standards. Those standards require that we plan and perform the audit to obtain sufficient, appropriate evidence to provide a reasonable basis for our findings and conclusions based upon our audit objectives. We believe that the evidence obtained provides a reasonable basis for our findings and conclusions based upon our audit objectives.

Appendix B
Management Comments to the Draft Report

U.S. Department of Homeland Security
Washington, DC 20528

Homeland
Security

July 18, 2014

MEMORANDUM FOR: The Honorable John Roth
                   Inspector General
                   Office of Inspector General

FROM: Jim H. Crumpacker, CIA, CFE
                   Director
                   Departmental GAO-OIG Liaison Office

SUBJECT: OIG Draft Report: "DHS Pandemic Preparedness"
                   (Project No. 13-155-AUD-DHS)

Thank you for the opportunity to review and comment on this draft report. The U.S. Department of Homeland Security (DHS) appreciates the Office of Inspector General's (OIG's) work in planning and conducting its review and issuing this report.

DHS agrees with the intent of all 11 recommendations outlined in the draft report. However, the Department is concerned that OIG has not appropriately characterized a number of issues discussed in the report, resulting in a misrepresentation of the information and evidence that DHS program officials and subject matter experts provided to the auditors during the audit, and of the DHS pandemic preparedness program in general. Specifically:

1. **The OIG seems to have overemphasized the final level of controls rather than viewing them in their role as last in a hierarchy of controls.** Personal protective equipment (PPE) and medical countermeasures (MCM) are the final levels of control available to the Department and are one part of a multi-level hierarchy. This hierarchy is a state-of-the-art occupational health principle, captured in American National Standards Institute (ANSI)/American Industrial Hygiene Association (AIHA) Z10-2012, "Occupational Safety and Health Management Systems," and summarized in Figure 1 below.[1] The concept is fundamental to Occupational Safety and Health Administration (OSHA) regulations and National Institute of Occupational Safety and Health training programs. This fundamental principle was utilized by the DHS Occupational Safety and Health Office and the DHS Office of Health Affairs (OHA) medical and occupational health professionals in developing pandemic response actions.

---

[1] MCM is equated to PPE in relative effectiveness and as a protective measure because it is administered AFTER a person actually is infected with a disease.

OIG-14-129

There are three applicable controls for the purpose of pandemic planning. These controls focus on limiting exposures first – by distancing personnel from sources of infection and using mechanical means such as barriers and ventilation to reduce potential contact with the infectious agent (known as engineering controls). The second level uses administrative controls including telework, shift rotation, vaccination programs, among other things, to reduce and provide a degree of protection to the population that may be exposed to infected co-workers or the public. The final level of controls, and least effective, from a business standpoint, as well as exposure reduction perspectives, includes PPE and MCM; sometimes these are all that can be reasonably provided for personnel that must perform higher-risk activities or who have become infected. There is not a single mention in the report of the two most important levels of controls and the effort the Department devoted to developing them, despite repeated discussions with OIG personnel in meetings and conversations. Exclusion of this principle overemphasizes the relative importance of the PPE and MCM controls.

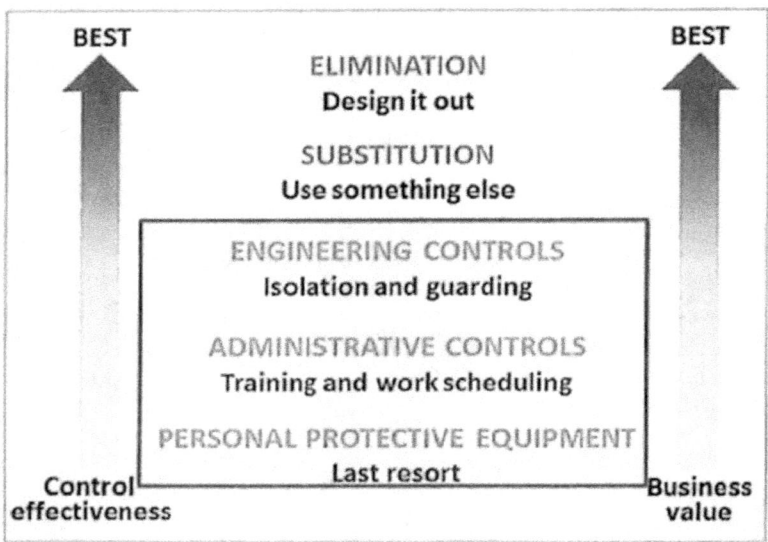

Figure 1: General Hierarchy of Controls, ANSI/AIHA Z10-2012, Occupational Safety and Health Management Systems. Controls applicable to pandemic planning are highlighted.

2. **OIG concluded that the Department has "no assurance it has sufficient personal protective equipment and antiviral medical countermeasures for a pandemic response" thus inhibiting DHS's ability to continue operations during a pandemic or ensure compliance with Department guidelines.** In fact, the Department is assured that it has sufficient PPE and antiviral MCMs. The OIG's conclusion seems to be reached by relying on the manufacturers' information rather than the judgment of published peer reviewed research, and DHS's highly experienced medical, safety, and health professionals with concurrence of subject matter experts from the U.S. Department of Health and Human Services (HHS), Centers for Disease Control and Prevention (CDC).

OIG-14-129

Both the PPE and MCM in the stockpiles audited have been tested and determined to be useable by DHS professional staff; this should not lead to the conclusion that there is no assurance that they are currently useable, and plans to replace these in upcoming years indicate the stocks are being managed, not allowed to become obsolete.

The PPE stockpile is very simple in nature: surgical-style nitrile gloves, surgical masks, and filtering facepiece disposable respirators. When these products were purchased, there were no established or published shelf life data, nor was shelf-life stated on the box or in the literature. When asked, the manufacturers stated that they tested them for five years, and as a result certified/guaranteed them for five years, but owners were told they could examine the products and determine if they were still useable based on visual inspection. The parts of these products that are most at risk are any flexible components; with exposure to heat, ultraviolet rays, and oxidation, the gloves, elastic headbands, and valves can become brittle or non-elastic. Filters and filter media are the most stable component of most filter facepiece respirators. Testing them is simply a matter of examining a random sample from stock in the same storage conditions and determining if they retain their flexibility.

The current PPE inventory is in useable condition at the time of this report, but with further aging it may not be useable in coming years. The manufacturers recently started placing firm 5-year expiration dates on respirator packaging; in the past users were told the respirators could be used after five years if they were inspected. Replacing the PPE by 2015 addresses concerns about it becoming unusable and also prevents regular trips to the warehouse to verify it is still intact. During a recent (spring 2014) inventory evaluation of the pandemic PPE stockpile, DHS offered this PPE to Components who use it regularly in daily operations, but little was requested; therefore most of these supplies must be placed in surplus when replaced. After this supply is replaced with new, there will be no inspection allowance and the PPE will have to be replaced after five years.

For MCM, the authority and expertise of the Food and Drug Administration (FDA) appears not to have been considered. The current stockpile of MCMs is part of an aggressive shelf-life extension program used by the FDA to analyze "outdated" MCMs and extend the original manufacturer's shelf life when they are shown to be still useable. This process conserves Departmental resources and establishes that the on-hand MCM are currently useable. Further, the Department provided DHS Components a copy of the most recent and relevant HHS guidance documenting that one or two courses of MCM were considered reasonable. Combined with coverage for the entire DHS workforce, critical contractors, and those in the Department's care and custody, it is unclear what the OIG considers sufficient.

Furthermore, the state of PPE and MCM supplies is not an appropriate indicator of pandemic readiness. As the last tools in a systematic hierarchy of controls, they are not the most efficient or effective means of maintaining workforce health. Despite this fact, PPE and MCM are commonly and erroneously viewed as the primary means of workforce protection, likely because they are more familiar to laypersons and they are more tangible and easily accounted for. The use of PPE also shifts much of the burden of

3

protection from the employer to the employee. Using PPE stock levels as an indicator of preparedness is based on a misconception that during a pandemic, the entire workforce should wear PPE, when in fact it will be determined by risk assessments and feasibility of other control methods.

OSHA requires agencies to perform pandemic risk analyses on their workforce and establish (due to work-related exposures) which risk level they fall under, ranging from low to very high. A risk analysis was completed by DHS during the H1N1 pandemic response and has recently been updated due to the new DHS plan. Based on risk assessments, DHS has only a limited number of personnel with risk assessments that recommend "mandatory PPE use" during a serious pandemic. Use is linked to specific activities that increase risk. The majority of these personnel already wear PPE regularly while performing their duties, so they are not expected to rely on pandemic stockpiles of PPE. The remaining employees, including almost all at the DHS Headquarters served by the PPE stockpile at the Federal Emergency Management Agency (FEMA) Cumberland warehouse, are termed by OSHA as "voluntary users," the lowest risk group. Employers are not required to provide any PPE to personnel in this low-risk group, and when they do, it is recognized in the standards that it is done both to help prevent a possible, but unlikely, exposure to the disease and to provide a degree of reassurance and comfort to the employee.

Similarly, the antiviral medications in the DHS stockpile are not vaccinations and do not prevent infection; they reduce the symptoms of an infected person and allow them to return to work earlier and provide an additional means of intervention when vaccines may not yet be developed or available in sufficient quantities. In cases where they are appropriate and effective for a given disease, they can provide a significant benefit when applied to a large workforce at times of high absenteeism and help ensure workforce coverage to continue mission essential functions. However, while employers were encouraged to stockpile antiviral MCM when used within the context of a broader occupational health strategy, there is no interagency mandate to provide antiviral MCM, but rather a determination of the Department leadership to enhance workforce availability and protection. Considering this, the on-hand goal of ensuring availability of MCM for all employees, contractors and those in the care and custody of DHS and the fact that the supplies available are currently useable do not support an implication of a readiness failure.

3. **The OIG incorrectly states that "about 81 percent of its [antiviral] stockpile will expire by the end of 2015 (shown in Table 1 of OIG's draft report)."** The Department provided OIG emails documenting that by July 1, 2013, the expiration dates of most of the current stockpile of antiviral MCM had already been extended according to criteria defined by the FDA, so that only 15 percent of DHS's antiviral stockpile is set to expire in 2015—an amount that DHS has budgeted to replace through purchase. An additional small percentage of antiviral stocks that have been returned from DHS Components following their deployment in response to the 2009 H1N1 Influenza pandemic may also be retired in 2015 because the small lot sizes do not meet the fiscal threshold for testing. The current stockpile of MCM is part of an aggressive shelf-life extension program

4

OIG-14-129

(SLEP) managed by OHA to analyze MCM and extend the original manufacturer's shelf life when they are determined to be still effective. Extending the shelf life of MCM is a responsible use of departmental resources providing significant cost deferrals and valuable time to smooth out replacement for the initial large MCM purchases made with one-time supplemental funding.

Additionally, many steps have been taken since the 2006 pandemic planning supplemental appropriation of $47 million to improve on the initial MCM planning. Specifically:

a. OHA has conducted five separate data calls from 2006 to 2013 to DHS Components to determine their specific MCM and PPE needs. DHS has used the results of these data calls to assess needs and make effective program management and purchasing decisions.

b. OHA developed methodologies for determining the MCM needs identified in the data calls, to include the amount of MCM needed to provide coverage, at the direction of the DHS Secretary's office, for the DHS workforce and all critical contractors and those in DHS care and custody.

c. OHA has conducted replenishment planning which has been captured in the budgeting process and other activities, such as pursuing shelf life extension opportunities.

DHS is more prepared than most federal agencies to provide MCM protection for its workforce. As the sole civilian Department with the only mature antiviral stockpile and dispensing program, DHS is working closely with CDC on the development of updated guidance for all federal departments and agencies.

4. **The report does not acknowledge the current state of affairs of DHS pandemic planning.** Beginning in March 2013, a working group consisting of DHS Headquarters and Operational Component representatives spent a significant amount of time and effort writing a Departmental Pandemic Workforce Protection Plan (PWPP). This PWPP, signed by the DHS Secretary in October 2013 – and subsequently provided to the audit team – outlines the total pandemic policy for DHS – from readiness measures including risk assessments and supply to actual response such as implementing the hierarchy of controls. This successful effort, along with the Component-specific plans and analyses it generated, should have been acknowledged in the audit report, as they were completed prior to the initiation of the audit, addressed many of the issues outlined in the report, and have a far greater effect on current DHS pandemic preparedness than irregularities in the stockpiles of PPE and MCM may have.

The draft report contained 11 recommendations with which the Department concurs. Specifically, OIG recommended:

Recommendation 1: That the Deputy Secretary identify and designate an office responsible for the management and accountability of pandemic PPE.

5

Response: Concur. The Office of the Under Secretary for Management designated the DHS Office of the Chief Readiness Support Officer as being responsible for the management and accountability of pandemic PPE effective January 2014. We request that OIG consider this recommendation resolved and closed.

Recommendation 2: That the Deputy Secretary develop a strategy for management, storage, and distribution of pandemic PPE.

Response: Concur. The DHS Chief Readiness Support Officer issued a Pandemic Logistics Support Plan Charter on May 30, 2014. This charter establishes the framework for the development of a Department pandemic logistics support plan for pandemic PPE. A Pandemic Logistics Integration Team (iTeam) has also been established with representation from DHS Components and pandemic PPE requirements have been drafted. Estimated Completion Date (ECD): September 30, 2014.

Recommendation 3: That the Deputy Secretary implement an inventory system for the current inventory and future inventories of pandemic PPE.

Response: Concur. Members of the Pandemic Logistics iTeam are reviewing the application of the Department's existing personal property inventory management systems for establishing management and inventory controls for pandemic PPE. The current pandemic PPE inventories are being distributed within DHS where operational requirements can be augmented; remaining items will be surplused in accordance with federal and Department requirements and standards. ECD: September 30, 2014.

Recommendation 4: That the Deputy Secretary work with components to establish a methodology for determining sufficient types and quantities of pandemic PPE to align with the department-wide pandemic plan.

Response: Concur. Work is underway. A workgroup has been established under the Pandemic Logistics iTeam to develop PPE requirements using an employee risk based approach supporting work place controls. ECD: September 30, 2014.

Recommendation 5: That the Deputy Secretary have components implement inventory control procedures for pre-positioned pandemic PPE to monitor stockpiles, track shipments, and ensure compliance with departmental guidance.

Response: Concur. This is in the planning stage. A policy and standards workgroup is being established under the Pandemic Logistics iTeam to establish PPE control procedures and standards. ECD: September 30, 2014.

Recommendation 6: That the DHS MCM Working Group and OHA determine requirements of antiviral MCM for the Department to maintain critical operations during a pandemic.

Response: Concur. OHA continues to solicit, receive, and address DHS component MCM needs and requirements as a standing agenda item during the monthly MCM Working Group

6

OIG-14-129

meeting, and as a key element of the MCM Quarterly Reports, OHA prepares and distributes as part of the MCM program. Additionally, DHS is working with CDC on an interagency process to define antiviral stockpiling needs on behalf of the entire federal government. We request that OIG consider this recommendation resolved and closed.

Recommendation 7: That OHA create an antiviral MCM Acquisition Management Plan to include:

a) A methodology for determining the ideal quantity of antiviral MCM OHA will stockpile and how frequently it will be reevaluated;
b) A replenishment plan; and
c) Inventory tracking, reporting, and reconciliation procedures for existing stockpile and new antiviral purchases.

Response: Concur. An MCM Integrated Logistics Support Program (ILSP) has been drafted and is currently in DHS clearance. Completion of the MCM ILSP will address all three elements of this recommendation. ECD: September 30, 2014.

Recommendation 8: That OHA revise procedures to ensure proper contract oversight by government employees for management of its MCM support service contracts and ensure the contracting officer's representatives follow procedures.

Response: Concur in principle. Existing procedures as described in the Homeland Security Acquisition Regulation, Homeland Security Acquisition Manual, the DHS Office of Procurement Operations Contracting Officer's Representative guidebook and component specific procedures addressing Contracting Officer Representative duties and responsibilities are adequate for ensuring proper contract oversight, but these procedures were not followed consistently in the administration of MCM support service contracts. Since OIG identified findings concerning inadequate oversight, OHA has taken steps to ensure that highly qualified contracting officer's representatives are assigned to all MCM support service contracts. These employees provide direct and comprehensive oversight of each aspect of the MCM project including detailed governance over all related contract support. We request that OIG consider this recommendation resolved and closed.

Recommendation 9: That OHA finalize and issue antiviral MCM guidance on the storage conditions, security, and distribution for antiviral MCM for all components.

Response: Concur. Storage and security guidance MCM standard operating procedures initially released in 2010 have been updated and expanded, and provided to Component MCM planners. They have also been posted to the DHS Connect Intranet MCM page. We request that OIG consider this recommendation resolved and closed.

Recommendation 10: That OHA finalize the antiviral MCM recall it has initiated on the CBP, ICE, FEMA, and USSS inventories.

7

Response: Concur. The recall is complete. OHA recently received a confirmation letter, dated July 7, 2014, from the HHS storage facility advising that all antiviral lots had been returned. We request that OIG consider this recommendation resolved and closed.

Recommendation 11: That OHA collaborate with CBP to determine the safety and effectiveness of the antibiotic MCM that have been stored alongside their antivirals.

Response: Concur. OHA continues to collaborate with all DHS Components to include U.S. Customs and Border Protection, through the MCM Working Group, to validate the safety and effectiveness of MCM. DHS employs the approved SLEP in close coordination with the FDA and the U.S. Department of Defense. To date, ten lots of antibiotic MCM have been submitted to SLEP for testing and of those for which testing has been completed all have been found to remain efficacious resulting in a cost avoidance of $5.1 million to the Department.

In addition to extending the shelf life, the SLEP testing verifies the safety/efficacy of MCM that may have been stored improperly (outside of the manufacturer's temperature range). In one instance, 5,450 bottles of antibiotics were exposed to a temperature spike over 100 degrees Fahrenheit for an unknown duration. The lot was submitted to SLEP in order to test for continued efficacy. It was found to be still safe and effective for use, and it was returned to the DHS stockpile.

Additionally, on July 7, 2014, OHA provided procedural guidance to DHS Components regarding MCM on measures to ensure the safety and effectiveness of medications – including antibiotics – in the MCM Program. We request that OIG consider this recommendation resolved and closed.

Again, thank you for the opportunity to review and provide comments on this draft report. Technical comments were previously provided under separate cover. Please feel free to contact me if you have any questions. We look forward to working with you in the future.

8

Appendix C
Major Contributors to This Report

Brooke Bebow, Director
Stephanie Christian, Audit Manager
Gary Crownover, Program Analyst
Ruth Gonzalez, Program Analyst
Matthew Noll, Program Analyst
Mark A. Phillips, Auditor
Melissa Prunchak, Program Analyst
Kevin Dolloson, Communications Analyst
Priscilla Cast, Referencer

Appendix D
Report Distribution

Department of Homeland Security

Secretary
Deputy Secretary
Chief of Staff
Deputy Chief of Staff
General Counsel
Executive Secretary
Director, GAO/OIG Liaison Office
Assistant Secretary for Office of Policy
Assistant Secretary for Office of Public Affairs
Assistant Secretary for Office of Legislative Affairs
Chief Privacy Officer

Office of Management and Budget

Chief, Homeland Security Branch
DHS OIG Budget Examiner

Congress

Congressional Oversight and Appropriations Committees, as appropriate

www.ingramcontent.com/pod-product-compliance
Lightning Source LLC
Chambersburg PA
CBHW081134280526
45787CB00007B/3079